CW00369645

THEY DIED TOO YOUNG

MALCOLM X

BY
Harry Adés

This edition first published by Parragon Books Ltd in 1995

Produced by
Magpie Books Ltd, London

Illustrations courtesy of: Rex Features; Associated Press.

ISBN 0 75250 715 X

A copy of the British Library Cataloguing in Publication
Data is available from the British Library.

Typeset by Hewer Text Composition Services, Edinburgh
Printed in Singapore by Printlink International Co.

THEY DIED TOO YOUNG
Malcolm X

Malcolm Little

'I learned early that crying out in protest could accomplish things.'

Only weeks before Malcolm was born, the infamous nightriders of the Ku Klux Klan, the most feared of the White supremacist groups, galloped up to the family home in Omaha, Nebraska. They surrounded the house, shotguns and rifles in hand, and demanded to see his father, Earl

Little. They planned to lynch him
there and then, in full view of his
family. Standing defiant in the doorway of their humble home, heavily
pregnant with Malcolm, Louise Little
shouted that she was alone in the
house with her three small children.
The riders warned them to leave,
because the White townsfolk would
no longer put up with her husband's
trouble-stirring among the 'good Negroes'. Frustrated, they rode around
the house smashing every window
with their rifle butts, their torches
lighting up the night sky.

Earl was a very tall, dark man with one
eye, an outspoken Baptist preacher,
who was never intimidated, especially
not by White racists. He had grown up

in Georgia, a Southern state beset by racial tension and violence. Three of his brothers had been murdered by Whites, so he had decided to spend his life as an activist, calling for Blacks to leave America and establish an independent nation in Africa. It was because of his position that he was targeted by the Klansmen.

Shortly after Malcolm was born on 19 May, 1925, the Little family moved north to Lansing, Michigan, hoping that the new area would be free from the violent racism of the South. However, the family's hopes were soon dashed. At four years old, Malcolm's first vivid memory was when night-riders again attacked his home. This time it was a hate group called 'the

Black Legion', who stalked the night in black robes, terrorizing Lansing. They had heard about Earl's attempts to start a Black rights organization, and had set fire to his house while the family lay sleeping inside.

Malcolm remembered being shaken awake into the confusion. The house was filled with smoke and flames, and pistol shots rang about him. Earl was firing at the Legionnaires as they sped off into the darkness, while his wife managed to snatch up the children, just making it into the yard, before the house crashed down in a shower of sparks and blistered wood. When the police and firemen came, they merely stood around, gloating at the spectacle. In fact the police made no attempt to catch the riders, but questioned Earl about the gun he had used to scare them away. Earl built a new home outside East Lansing, but the police often raided it, searching for the gun. It had been sewn up inside a pillow, and was never discovered.

Times were very hard, and the best jobs a Black man could hope for would be as a waiter or shoeshine boy. Malcolm remarked that his family were so poor that they 'would eat the hole out of a doughnut'. But they were better off than many of the urban Blacks. The money raised in collections at the end of Earl's services went on the family, and their modest plot of land enabled them to keep chickens and turkeys, and grow a few vegetables. During the Great

Depression, many desperate, poverty-stricken Blacks turned to the fiery preaching of Earl as a voice of hope. Malcolm loved the feeling of pride that the services gave him, and for a time was happy. But it was not long before disaster struck the family again.

One afternoon in 1931, following an argument with his wife, Earl stormed out of the house and disappeared. Louise, who had visions of her husband's death, could not control her tears when he had not returned by bedtime. Malcolm remembered being woken up by his mother's screams when police came to take her to the hospital. All the children knew something terrible must have happened to their father. In hospital, Louise was too afraid to look beneath the sheet where Earl lay. He had been so savagely beaten that half his skull had been crushed. Friends were sure that the Black Legion had battered him unconscious and then dumped his body on tramtracks to die. His body had been cut almost in half. Incredibly, Earl lay in hospital for two and a half hours in that condition, before his stubborn will to survive finally broke. The police did not even look for his murderers.

Earl Little's death left Louise to look after eight children without protector or provider. For a while, they were able to get by with money from a life insurance policy. But a second, larger policy refused to make any payments on the grounds that he had committed

suicide. Louise and her friends pro-
tested against the ridiculous excuse,
but in vain. She never saw the money
she was owed. When funds ran out,
Malcolm's family strained to make
ends meet.

The welfare cheque was never enough
to pay outstanding credit at the gro-
cery, and Louise's strong sense of pride
stopped her from receiving charity.
Sometimes, they survived on corn-
meal mush or boiled dandelion
greens. At school the children were
taunted for eating 'fried grass'. In 1934,
at the height of the Depression, the
family's solidarity began to disinte-
grate. The welfare agents became in-
creasingly intrusive, asking Louise why
she refused gifts for the family, and

why Malcolm's skin was so much lighter than the others' (Louise alleged that her mother had been raped by a White man). Malcolm had been spending more and more time away from home: in the morning he would steal food from shops, and at dinner-time he would 'accidentally' drop in for a meal with the Gohannas family, who had a nephew of about his age. Time and again he was caught for stealing, and the welfare people succeeded in taking him away from his family. He was relieved to find that the Gohannases had agreed to take him in; they enjoyed his company, and Malcolm won some respite from the unbearable tensions and pressures on his family.

In 1937, Louise was jilted by a man from Lansing whom she thought might marry her, and this blow proved to be too much for her ailing sanity. She would sit around the house for hours on end, or walk and talk aimlessly as if her children were no longer there. The welfare agents seized their chance quickly, and she was committed to a mental hospital, where she remained for the next twenty-six years. Malcolm understandably felt bitter that the state had managed to break up the family. Often his emotions would run over, causing him to disrupt lessons at school. He was soon expelled.

He was sent to a juvenile detention centre in Mason, about twelve miles

from his home town. Malcolm reacted
well to his new environment: it was
the first time in his life that he had his
own room. He did what was expected
of him, and very soon became the
directors' favourite. Although they
were good to him, they would often
make racist comments in front of him
without even being aware that they
were doing so. Nevertheless, they got
on well together, and Malcolm was
enrolled at Mason Junior High, the
local school. Free from the burden of
his family, his schoolwork steadily
improved. He was always in the top
three of his class, and by the end of the
year he was so popular that he was
voted class president. Yet, his success
and happiness were only superficial, as
he was troubled with the attitude of his

Malcolm X

Conditions in rural America were very poor
during the Depression

classmates. His friends called him 'nigger' without realizing the hurt it was causing, and since he was almost the only Black in the school, he felt that they looked on him as some exotic novelty, not as an equal.

In 1940, Malcolm's half-sister, Ella, one of Boston's successful business-women and socialites, came to visit her needy relatives in Michigan. She quickly struck up a friendship with young Malcolm and invited him to stay with her that summer. The trip proved to be a turning-point. He was mesmerized by the sights, sounds and smells of the big city. On every street corner were the best-dressed people he had ever seen; jukeboxes blared out the tunes of his favourites, like Duke

Ellington; and the restaurants wafted into the streets the smells of 'rich, greasy, down-home Black cooking'. He marvelled at Ella's house in the richest part of Roxbury, the Black area of Boston. Never before had he experienced such luxury and privilege.

Malcolm was an intelligent and ambitious boy, but his hopes were needlessly dashed by the very people who should have offered encouragement. When summer came to an end, and he had to return to Mason, he could not get the wonders of Boston out of his mind. Back at school, Malcolm told one of his favourite teachers that he wanted to be a lawyer. He was told, in all earnest, 'A lawyer – that's no realistic goal for a nigger . . . Why don't you plan on carpentry?' Shortly afterwards, Malcolm drew away from White people, and gave up his school-work. He wrote to Ella every other day, pleading with her to let him stay in Boston. Somehow the welfare department agreed on the transfer, and before long he was on a Greyhound bus to the city.

Detroit Red

'A man should do anything that he was slick enough, or bad and bold enough, to do.'

When Malcolm arrived in Roxbury, he described himself as a 'hick': a lanky fifteen-year-old, fresh from the country, his hair ungreased, his gangling ankles and wrists jutting awkwardly out of a cheap green suit several sizes too small for him. Before settling

down to work, Ella advised him to
look around the town and get a feel for
it, since he may not get such chances
again. Malcolm was immediately at-
tracted to the 'town' section of the
ghetto, as he felt that the people living
in Ella's area were 'snotty Blacks'
affecting White airs and graces. It
upset Ella that Malcolm did not spend
more time in the Hill neighbourhood
with 'nice young people his age', but
Malcolm could not tear himself away
from the world of cheap restaurants,
poolrooms, bars, storefront churches,
pawnshops, and the sharply dressed
'cats' who hung about on the corners
all day. He did not want to upset Ella,
so he decided to surprise her by
finding a job for himself. Looking
for a 'slave' (ghetto slang for a job),

he met Shorty in a seedy poolhall. Shorty, it turned out, was also from Lansing in Michigan. He took Malcolm, whom he nicknamed 'Red' because of his coppery hair, under his wing as a 'homeboy', and soon found him work as a shoeshine boy in the Roseland State Ballroom, one of the city's top music and dance venues.

Although Ella disapproved, there was no stopping Malcolm. The job let him hear and meet the best jazz musicians in the country every day – under segregation laws, his Black peers only had access twice a month. He was quick to learn his trade, and found that the White customers gave him larger tips if he acted up his 'Blackness', and bowed his head in deference. But most of his money came from the 'hustle': selling cannabis, and putting punters in touch with local prostitutes. His proximity to these vices soon led him to enjoy them also, and although 'country', he was happy to be accepted by Shorty and his friends. Malcolm wanted to look the part too, and decided to shed his gawky green suit. He bought, on credit, a sky-blue zoot suit, which featured trousers thirty inches at the knee but a tight twelve inches at the ankle, and a long jacket that pinched his waist but flared out below his knees. Shorty decided that Malcolm's hair had grown long enough to 'conk'. By pouring Devil lye onto the scalp, the hair straightens, while the scalp burns. In years to come, Malcolm would see his conk hairstyle as his 'first really big step toward self-degradation'. He could not bear to think that he endured the burning lye on his head just to make him look a little more like a White man. At the time, of course his conk and zoot suit made him a 'hip cat', a streetwise hustler looking for action.

While he was at the Roseland State Ballroom, he picked up a wild dance called the Lindy Hop. He packed in his job, because he wanted to dance more than work in the evenings. Ella found him a respectable day-job as a soda-fountain clerk, where he met, to his half-sister's great delight, a well-mannered young girl, Laura. Malcolm

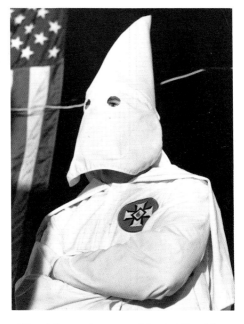

The sinister appearance of the Ku Klux Klan

Racial discrimination was blatant in
the 1950s

thought she was the best dancing part-
ner he had ever had. But, after only a
couple of dates, and at the end of a
'showtime' session, when the most agile
and acrobatic dancers take the floor to
show off to the rest of the clubbers, he
was approached by Sophia, a White,
who had been dazzled by his energetic
'hopping'. Malcolm dumped Laura
there and then, in favour of the White
girl, whom he paraded in front of his
friends as the highest status symbol.
Even Shorty got some credit for Malcolm's catch, since he was the one who
had 'schooled' him.

With Sophia he spent his nights driv-
ing around from dance to dance, and
bar to bar. The next time that Malcolm
saw Laura, however, she was a

destroyed woman. She had left home
and school, and, now notorious
around Roxbury, fed her dope addic-
tion by selling her body. Malcolm
never forgave himself.

Ella was anxious to get Malcolm away
from Sophia, and since so many men
had been drafted for the War, jobs
opened up for him in New York, a
city he had long dreamed about. Malcolm, lying about his age, found work
selling sandwiches on the 'Yankee
Clipper' train, which ran between
Boston and New York. He was able
to visit the Big Apple between runs
and on his first visit he was entranced
by the cool customers at the popular
bar, Small's Paradise, who sat un-
stirred, so unlike his loudmouth

Boston friends who flashed about what little money they had. He later remarked, 'Within the first five minutes in Small's, I had left Boston and Roxbury for ever.'

If there was one thing that tied Malcolm's varied life together, it was his boundless energy for things that interested him. He worked so hard at his job that he picked up the nickname 'Sandwich Red' from his contemporaries. Intoxicated partly by the emotions that New York excited in him, but mostly from the reefers that kept him high, he ran up and down the train shouting at the passengers and hurling abuse at those who would not buy from him. Most of all, he hated the soldiers. One time, a 'big,

beefy, red-faced cracker' (slang for a
serviceman), reeking of bourbon and
reeling from Malcolm's torrential
swearing, staggered to his feet and
roared, 'I'm going to fight you, nigger!' Unruffled, Malcolm just laughed
in his face and coolly said, 'Sure, I'll
fight, but you've got too many clothes
on.' The army man struggled to get his
heavy greatcoat off, while Malcolm
stood in front of him, giggling that
he still had too many clothes on.
Before long, the soldier had stripped
to his underpants, and the whole
carriage was crying with laughter
around him. His dejected friends led
the humiliated beefcake away, and
Malcolm, the victor, continued with
his trade.

Nevertheless, it was no way to treat customers, and Malcolm lost his job. He had just turned seventeen when he found work as a waiter at Small's Paradise, a heaven to him. He loved his new job so much that he arrived an hour before his shift each day, just to hear the fantastic stories of the hustlers who frequented the place. Malcolm, always quick to learn, absorbed every drop of information like a sponge. He was schooled well by such experts as Fewclothes, an old pickpocket, Jumpsteady, a nimble cat burglar, and West Indian Archie, one of the most dangerous gambling racketeers in the ghetto. Soon he knew the tricks of hustles like the numbers (a gambling game), pimping, confidence tricks, peddling drugs, even armed robbery. He found out how to sell damaged goods as though they were priceless antiques, where to hide drugs so that the police would never find them, and how to force money out of reluctant debtors. From the prostitutes, he learned about the perverse differences between the White and Black man's sexual preferences. He made many friends in the underworld, and they regarded the enthusiastic youngster with fondness too. They gave him the name 'Detroit Red' because of his Michigan past and his bright-red conk hairstyle. In fact, the notorious Forty Thieves Gang made him a present of an expensive, dark blue designer-suit – stolen, of course.

In Boston, Malcolm Little spent much of his
time in dance halls

Malcolm was entranced by New York

The bar rules did not allow any hustling of any kind, and Malcolm stayed clean for some time to keep his job. But he broke a criminal's cardinal law by 'trying a hustle' on a serviceman. Penalties in wartime were harsh against anyone considered trying to 'impair the morals' of a soldier, and Malcolm should have known better. He asked a lonely-looking army man if he needed a woman to cheer him up, and played right into the hands of a military spy. He was lucky that he was not charged, but he would be under surveillance from now on, so was barred from Small's Paradise.

Malcolm knew that if he was going to survive he would have to start a hustle. He and his friend, Sammy the Pimp, decided that his best chance lay in the drugs racket, Malcolm himself already being a prolific user. Sammy lent him a 'stake' – enough money to get started – and Malcolm soon found that he could make quick money peddling hashish to his musician friends. He scarcely slept as he rushed to wherever the musicians congregated, selling reefers 'like a wild man'; and best of all, for the first time in his life he felt free.

But he would have to be careful to keep his newly won freedom. His prodigious sales had alerted the New York narcotics squad to his dealing. Being caught in possession would certainly mean a jail sentence. To beat the police, he carried his dope in a small package inside his coat, under his armpit. If he smelt trouble he would walk through a doorway, or round a corner, and loosen his arm until the packet dropped. By night, when he sold most, the trick was hard to spot, and he could always return to the drop-point if mistaken. Many of Harlem's detectives were frustrated by his ruse. When he found that the police had searched his room, he suspected that they had planted drugs to catch him. Taking no chances, he left the apartment for good, and started to carry a gun. Kept wedged beneath his belt and in the small of his back, he knew the police never looked there during a routine frisking. But his hustle became more and more difficult as the police closed in.

Eventually, he moved to another pre-
cinct, the poorest in the ghetto, where
most of the addicts were. But this area
was so full of the most parasitical
creatures in New York that he did
not last long there either. Malcolm
said that they had the 'instincts of
animals' and living there was 'truly
the survival of the fittest'. They were
quick to learn his strategy. Jumping
out of doorways at Malcolm, he would
drop his packet, which they would
snatch up 'like a chicken on corn'.
Soon, he was in debt and in need of
another plan. His friend, Sammy the
Pimp, had a brainwave. He could use
his old railway worker's pass to travel
the East Coast for nothing, and supply
his musician friends with all the hashish they could smoke as they moved

from one venue to the next. Further-
more, it would keep him out of the
eyes of the Harlem police. It worked
like a dream.

However, Malcolm's paradise of fast
money, drugs, and friendship with
America's top musicians was threa-
tened by the War. Shortly after
Malcolm's eighteenth birthday, the
New York draft board had finally
tracked him down. There were only
three things in Malcolm's world that
scared him: jail, a job, and the army.
He knew exactly what he had to do
to stay out of the clutches of the latter:
pretend to be as mad as a hatter.
Whenever he sensed there were
army spies about, he would yell that
he would love to join up – with the

Japanese Army. On the day of the interview, he wore his most outrageous zoot suit, complemented by yellow knob-toe shoes, and, of course, his bright red conk. He burst in 'skipping and tipping', and shouted as loud and long as he could in his heaviest street-slang. The long line of draftees stared on in shocked silence, while the officials watched open-mouthed. All the time, he was making it sound as though he was the most eager soldier-to-be that they would ever find: 'Crazy-o, daddy-o,' he yelled, 'get me moving. I can't wait to get in that brown . . .' Not surprisingly, he soon found himself in the office of the army psychiatrist. The shrink sat there unmoved for five minutes before he even spoke, just doodling on his pad and listening to Malcolm's crazy talk. Malcolm realized that he would have to pull out all the stops for this one. He kept jerking round, looking over his shoulder as if some unseen presence might be listening. As quick as a flash, he leapt up and checked the doors of the room, including the cupboard door, for invaders. When the coast was clear, he bent double and whispered hard and fast in the shrink's ear, 'Don't you tell nobody . . . I want to get sent down South. Organize them nigger soldiers, you dig? Steal us some guns and kill up crackers!' The pencil dropped from the psychiatrist's hand as he stared at the madman, who looked like he might suck the bulging, disbelieving eyes from the doctor's sockets. 'That will be all,' was the superior's strangled, almost inaudible reply. Malcolm never did find out why the army rejected him.

Hustler

'Everybody in Harlem needed some kind of hustle to survive, and needed to stay high in some way to forget what they had to do to survive.'

The days of his railway drug-pushing came to an end when he was caught in a locker room at Grand Central Station in a big-money poker game. The police barred him from the station, and he lost his job on the trains. He was back on the streets of Harlem, only this time he could not do his usual hustle – the dope squad were far too familiar with him. Like a true hustler, uneducated and unskilled, he would have to live on his wits and cunning, risking anything and exploiting anyone. With his options closing down, Malcolm turned to armed robbery. He always carried one gun simply as 'street wear'. For work, he had much larger weapons, such as a Magnum. He needed help to prepare for a stick-up, and found nothing better than cocaine. It was the only drug left with a strong enough kick to get him in the mood. Soon enough, he was hooked, and a drug-induced paranoia made him change his room every couple of days, so fearful was he of capture.

New York club life, a scene from the film *Malcolm X*

Malcolm learnt to hustle on the streets of Harlem

On a bungled heist with Sammy the Pimp, he was very nearly caught. As they made their getaway, someone spotted them and police cars were on the scene in seconds. Thinking quickly, they stopped running. As a police car skidded to a halt near by, they jumped out into the street, hailing it to ask for directions. The policemen, who had thought that the men were going to give information, sped on in fury.

On another botched job, security guards fired on the duo, grazing Sammy. When the heat had cooled, Malcolm went to Sammy's apartment, and was greeted by his girlfriend, beside herself with rage. Blaming Malcolm for Sammy's wound, she clawed, bit, and kicked him, until he 'shut her up' with a punch to the face. Sammy went for his gun to teach him once and for all how to treat his ladies, but Malcolm escaped.

Losing friends, and seriously addicted to hard drugs, Malcolm was making a rapid descent into the gutter of Harlem. He drifted from hustle to hustle while the underworld tightened its grip on him. After an armed robbery at a bar, which had not involved him, a description of the robber made him a prime suspect. Heavies, hired by the bar's manager, broke into his apartment and roughed him up. The consequences could have been worse, but, luckily for Malcolm, another Harlem 'Red' confessed days later. A similar thing happened when 'a tall, light-skinned Negro' held up a craps game. This time a gang of Italian mobsters were told to kill him. They found him in a bar, and, just as one of them fumbled to get a gun out of his pocket, a policeman walked through the door. The would-be assassins had to make a dash for it, and Malcolm's life was once again spared.

But he was by no means in the clear. That day, Malcolm heard that West Indian Archie, one of the most feared men in the neighbourhood, was also after his blood. West Indian Archie thought that Malcolm had cheated him on the numbers game and gave him twelve hours to get back the money he was owed. Malcolm was truly scared. He later said, 'No one who wasn't ready to die messed with West Indian Archie.' The money was not the problem – Malcolm could have paid it quite easily. But if it could be shown that a hustler could be bluffed, or cracked under pressure, then he lost all respect in the ghetto. Malcolm had reached an impasse: to keep his hustler's honour, he would have to have a showdown with West Indian Archie.

The numbers racketeer caught up with Malcolm in a bar. Doped up on cocaine, Malcolm was unaware that he had come in. Before he knew it, West Indian Archie had a gun against his head, and was cursing him wildly. He realized he would have to shoot his

Harlem residents campaign for better housing

Malcolm X made the Holy Pilgrimage to Mecca in 1964

way out, and tried to ease his .32 from
under his belt. West Indian Archie
sensed this immediately: 'You're
thinking you're going to kill me first,
Red. But I'm sixty. I'm an old man.
I've been to Sing Sing. My life is over.
You're a young man. Kill me, you're
lost anyway. All you can do is go to
prison.'

He was sure one of them had to die.
Luckily, West Indian Archie's friends,
smelling bloodshed, called him gently
to one side. Trying to keep his cool,
Malcolm slowly got off his stool. He
went outside the bar, and waited, hand
on gun, for five minutes for West
Indian Archie to show. He did not
appear, and Malcolm walked away.

Frightened out of his wits, he blitzed himself on a cocktail of drugs, including opium, cannabis, benzedrine and cocaine. By the time he woke up, he had well overstepped West Indian Archie's deadline. People in the streets steered clear of him. He had enough sense to drop his gun, knowing that the police would have got wind of the showdown. Sure enough, only moments later he was thoroughly frisked. They warned him to leave town, if he wanted to stay alive. With West Indian Archie, the Italian gangsters and the police all after his skin, he knew something had to give. Minutes later, someone called his name. He spun round, nerves jangling. It was his old friend Shorty from Boston. Word had even reached the Roxbury hustlers that Malcolm was in a corner, and Shorty had come to bail him out. Malcolm later said that this was his luckiest break.

However, he did not stay out of trouble in Boston either. On the contrary, he formed a burglary ring with Shorty, his old girlfriend Sophia (whom he had still been seeing in New York, even though she was now married), and a few trustworthy others. To make it clear to his new gang that he was the boss, he placed a single bullet in his gun, twirled the cylinder, and pressed the shaft against his temple. He pulled the trigger and the gun clicked. Again he pulled the trigger, but only the sound of the hammer on an empty chamber. His friends around him were shouting and screaming for him to stop. Yet again he pulled the trigger. Nothing. His eyes intense with emotion, he hissed, 'Never cross a man not afraid to die . . . now let's get to work.' Clearly, Malcolm was not afraid of anything – least of all, getting what he wanted.

For a while, the burglaries went very well. Sophia and her sister would pretend to be college girls doing a survey. In the houses they would make a note of all the valuables, and a rough plan of the building. During the following weeks, Shorty and Malcolm would do the job, while another had the getaway car ready. The gang members made enough to live the good life for weeks on end, and Malcolm was able to feed his drug habit. But it did not last. In fact, Malcolm blamed his final mistake on the muddled state his drugged-up mind was in. He had taken a stolen watch into a jeweller's to replace a broken crystal. Unfortunately for him, the watch was very special and all the jewellers in Boston had been notified of its disappearance. When he came to pick it up, the police were waiting for him. He went without a struggle and all but one of the gang members were rounded up.

In court, he and Shorty were given unusually large sentences on fourteen separate counts. Malcolm believed that they were really being punished for leading the good, White girls astray. Even his lawyer said, 'You had no business with White girls!'

Malcolm was sentenced for eight to ten years in Charlestown State Prison. By the time he was behind bars, he was only twenty, and had not even begun shaving. With hindsight, Malcolm was sure that the events leading up to his arrest were the will of Allah. And he could be forgiven for thinking this: for, in prison, he was to undergo a most spectacular transformation.

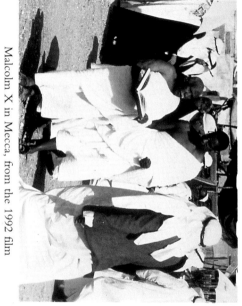

Malcolm X in Mecca, from the 1992 film

Friday 9 AM - April 25, 1964

هيئة بجدة المسلمة الكبرى

Dear Alex Haley:

I have just completed my pilgrimage
(Hajj) to the Holy City of Mecca, the Holiest
City in Islam, which is absolutely forbidden
for non-believers even to rest their eyes
upon. There were over 200,000 pilgrims
there, at the same time. This pilgrimage
is to the Muslim, as important as is going
to "heaven" to the Christian. I doubt if there
have been more than ten Americans to
ever make this pilgrimage. I know of
only two others who have actually made the
Hajj (and both of them are West Indian). Mr.
Muhammad and two of his sons made what
is known as "Omra" (the pilgrimage or "visit"
to Mecca outside of the Hajj season). I think
I'm the first American born Negro to make
the actual Hajj --- and if I'm not the

A letter from Malcolm X to the author
Alex Haley

From Satan to Savant

'I'd put prison second to college as the best place for a man to go if he needs to do some thinking.'

As a 'fish' (prison slang for new inmate), Malcolm certainly felt out of his depth. Until he knew the guards well enough to buy drugs from them, Malcolm suffered badly from withdrawal. It was a very tough prison, styled after the Bastille, with dirty, cramped cells and a covered bucket for a latrine, shared by a whole row of inmates. Malcolm was evil-tempered, angry with all around him, even his relatives on the outside. He refused to answer by his number when guards called him, and consistently ended up in solitary, where he would pace his cage, cursing everything, especially The Bible and God. To his peers, he became known as 'Satan'.

Only one man in his year at Charlestown made any impression on him. This was Bimbi, an old-time burglar, who had made great use of his many years locked up. Known as 'the library's best customer', his knowledge and eloquence commanded total respect among the prisoners and guards alike. Bimbi once flattened Malcolm's raving attacks against the Church, without ever using a foul word. But he saw that Malcolm had brains, and encouraged him to take up some correspondence courses. Malcolm was deeply affected by the way authoritative and skilled speaking could dominate an audience. Malcolm decided to take up English, Latin and penmanship – he could barely write by the time the streets had finished with him.

After a few months at a prison in Concord, Massachusetts, Ella managed to get him transferred to nearby Norfolk Prison Colony, an experimental rehabilitation centre. As prisons went, it was one of the most enlightened in the country. Many of

the inmates enjoyed intellectual pur-
suits, and instructors came from many
universities, including Harvard. A mil-
lionaire had left his entire library to the
prison, and inmates were allowed to
saunter up and down its aisles, choos-
ing books from the thousands available. Malcolm read keenly.

At about the same time, Malcolm had
received an unusual message from his
younger brother, Reginald: 'Don't eat
any more pork, and don't smoke any
more cigarettes. I'll show you how to
get out of prison.' Reginald had spent
a short period in the ghetto hustling
with his brother, and Malcolm immediately followed his advice, convinced
that he had a 'hype' to get him out.
But when Reginald made the long-

awaited visit, his advice was plain and simple: leave the ranks of the brain-washed Blacks behind, join the Nation of Islam, and follow Allah against 'the White devil'. Malcolm was stunned. He racked his brains, thinking of all the Whites he had met in his life. To him, all had been devils.

Reginald visited regularly when he saw the effect he had had on Malcolm. His brothers and sisters, also converted to the Nation of Islam, began to write to him from Michigan. They urged him to follow the teachings of 'The Honourable Elijah Muhammad', whom they believed to be the Messenger of Allah. Writing daily, they taught him the Nation's bizarre beliefs about the origins of

mankind. According to Elijah Muhammad, in the beginning there were
only Black people. Twenty-four wise
scientists ruled. They founded highly
advanced civilizations, sculptured the
natural world, created the moon, and
still had time to communicate with
nine-foot giants on Mars. Sixty thousand years ago, 'the big-head scientist'
Mr Yacub, who was born to create
trouble, break the peace and kill, was
exiled from the Holy City, Mecca.
Embittered, he used his knowledge
of genetics to produce an evil, schem-
ing, vicious race to wreak revenge –
the devil White race. The original
Black people herded them up and
confined them to the wastelands and
caves of Europe. Allah tried to civilize
the White savages by sending them

Malcolm X speaking at a campaign meeting

Malcolm X was prepared to die for his cause

Moses and Jesus, but they only succeeded in corrupting the prophets'
messages, spawning Judaism and
Christianity. It was written that the
Whites would rule for six thousand
years, enslaving millions of Blacks;
they would transport them to the
Americas where the Black people
would lose their language and cul-
ture, and be brainwashed into thinking
that Whites were superior. But a new
age was dawning. A man named W.D.
Fard had been born to lead the Black
race back to its former greatness. Fard,
who claimed to be the Islamic Mes-
siah, was Elijah Muhammad's tutor.

To Malcolm, the history was a revelation. It kindled in him a flame of pride
in being Black, and gave him hope that

the oppression he had experienced would soon end. Inspired by the prophecy of redemption, he embraced the new religion and was taken by Muhammad into the fold of the Nation of Islam. Like all the other members, he took the surname 'X', which symbolized the true African family-name that he could never know.

Driven by his new cause and the urge to write coherently to his new master, Elijah Muhammad, he embarked on a stringent programme of self-improvement. To better his vocabulary and hand writing, he began to copy every word out of a dictionary. He took up studies in history, religion, science, archaeology, philosophy, Greek and

Latin, and even dabbled in philology. The more he learned, the more he wanted to learn: there were simply not enough hours in the day to read. After the guards turned the lights out at ten, Malcolm X would strain to read by the dim glow of the corridor until four in the morning. His overworked eyes soon needed glasses.

It was six years since the young, doped-up delinquent had been thrown inside, and the parole board was so impressed by his total transformation that it granted him release. By the time he walked through the prison gates, he regarded his underworld life as though it had been somebody else's. True enough: for those who knew him, he was a different person.

Out of the Ashes

'All Negroes are angry and I am the angriest of them all.'

Malcolm X knew better than to go back to his old haunts in New York and Boston. His family found him a job in Detroit at a furniture shop. He worked hard and, whenever he could, he went to the Nation of Islam's Temple Number One where he immersed himself in their rituals. At last he had found a Black

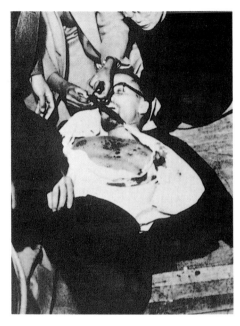

Malcolm X lies dying

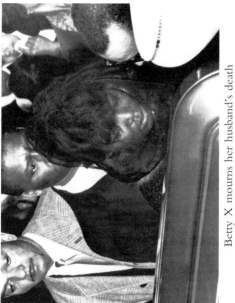

Betty X mourns her husband's death

community which was proud of its colour, and he felt that his fellows walked the streets radiating dignity and love. More than anything, Malcolm X wanted to spread this well-being and enlighten the brainwashed Blacks of the ghettos. As always, favouring action, he went to the poolhalls, bars and street corners using slang to get the message through. Many shied away from him, thinking him crazy, but he would not give up. In fact, he would talk in the ghettos until his voice was hoarse. After a few months of 'fishing' on the streets, he had tripled the congregation of the Detroit temple. His hard work earned him Elijah Muhammad's recognition. In the summer of 1953, he was made assistant minister to the temple.

Malcolm X worked hard to develop his speaking style, electrifying audiences with his witty tirades against Whites, his brazen-faced audacity and canny observations. 'We didn't land on Plymouth Rock, my brothers and sisters,' he thundered, 'Plymouth Rock landed on us!' After single-handedly starting a temple in Boston, and helping found three others in Massachusetts, Malcolm X earned promotion. As the up-and-coming star of the Nation, Elijah Muhammad made him minister of Temple Number Seven in New York. Home to over a million Blacks, here was enormous potential for conversions to the Nation. Under his dynamic leadership and outstanding ability to pull the crowds, membership rapidly grew.

Inexhaustible, Malcolm X preached every night, and travelled the country giving lessons about Islam. The organization, powered largely by his extraordinary energy, spread as far as the West Coast, with temples in Los Angeles and San Francisco. Despite its success, however, many of America's leaders had never even heard of the Nation of Islam. But, one evening in April, 1957, a small event thrust it into the public eye.

That night, in Harlem, the police came to break up a fight. When they told the crowd to move on, two members of Temple Number Seven, who were watching, refused to leave. The police did not tolerate this insolence and attacked one of the Muslims, Johnson

Hinton, coshing him savagely about the head until his scalp split open. When Hinton was arrested and thrown in a cell, Malcolm X was notified. He gathered up the Fruit of Islam, the highly disciplined military corps of the organization, and marched on the station, to ensure Hinton was getting medical treatment. Malcolm X and his troops remained in formation outside, silent and motionless, until their demands had been met. The eerie spectacle soon gathered a large and ugly crowd, tired of the years of police brutality. Afraid that there would shortly be a riot, the police chief ordered an ambulance for Hinton, but the crowd followed it to hospital and waited until they heard he was receiving adequate care. When it was clear that Hinton was all right, Malcolm signalled to the crowd, which dispersed. The incident made the national press, and the police department reassessed the power of the organization. The Nation and Hinton later sued the police department for brutality. The $70,000 payout made Malcolm X an overnight hero for the Blacks, and soon everyone in the ghetto was discussing the Muslims.

Malcolm X had a personal triumph in 1958. He had always mistrusted women since his hustling days. But his character had reformed enough for him to propose to Betty X. They had a very informal marriage in Detroit, and eventually had five daughters. He cherished the short times they had together, but as the voice of Black rage he was hardly ever at home.

By 1959, racial discrimination was the hottest issue in America. White Americans had been deeply shaken by a documentary 'The Hate That Hate Produced', which featured Black Muslims, such as Malcolm X, voicing their contempt for Whites. It showed how anger in the ghettos was near flashpoint. Very quickly, there was demand from all quarters of White society to find out more about the Nation, the angriest Black group in the country. Elijah Muhammad had developed a severe asthmatic condition and was too ill to make appearances, so he chose Malcolm X as his spokesman. He was invited to numerous television shows, and interviewed by pressmen from all over the world. They loved him because his flamboyant and controversial manner never failed to make sensational headlines.

Frustrated by the slow progress that Martin Luther King jun was making with his non-violent approach to reform, more and more Blacks turned to Malcolm X as their champion. He wanted changes 'by any means necessary' and strongly urged his followers to buy rifles to defend themselves. The media represented him as a demagogue and extremist, whipping up fear in Whites, and respect and love in many urban Blacks. By the early

1960s, Malcolm X was heading enormous rallies, attended by tens of thousands. He was a deft manipulator of a crowd's emotions. At one Harlem rally, he made a crowd so angry, that he thought he might have a bloody riot on his hands. He asked for silence and that the crowd disperse, and almost instantly it did. This gave him the reputation as the only man in America who could start or stop a race riot. Malcolm X just said, 'I don't know if I could start one. I don't know if I'd want to stop one.'

But his meteoric rise was met with jealousy by some Muslims close to Elijah Muhammad. They fed Muhammad's paranoia with stories that Malcolm X would turn against him, and cause trouble for the Nation. On the surface, Muhammad continued to reward Malcolm X for his work, making him the group's first National Minister, but he had already ordered his assassination. Followers faithful to Malcolm X informed him of their orders to kill him. At the same time, Malcolm X's faith in Muhammad was shattered by the revelation that he had been having a series of affairs with his secretaries and had sired illegitimate children. Malcolm X could not believe he had been so betrayed by Muhammad's breach of the Muslim's strict moral code. This upset him far more than the death threats, since he had always maintained he was willing to die for Muhammad.

After John F. Kennedy's assassination on 22 November 1963, Malcolm X told reporters the murder was 'a case of the chickens coming home to roost', meaning that the Whites were suffering from a climate of violence of their own creation. The comment outraged America's grieving masses, and gave Muhammad the opportunity he needed to isolate him from the Islamic community. He was suspended from the organization for ninety days. His Muslim friends warned him that reconciliation with Muhammad was impossible, but they would follow him if he decided to break away. In March 1964, he announced his split from the Nation of Islam to found his own revolutionary organization, Muslim Mosque, Incorporated. It was too dangerous for him to start recruiting then; if he stayed in New York, he knew he would be killed. He decided it was time to leave the country for a while. However, all the money he had made from public appearances had been given to the Nation, and he had hardly a penny to his name. Ella, helping Malcolm yet again, found enough money for him to fulfil a Muslim's ultimate duty: the Holy Pilgrimage to Mecca.

Martyr

*'It's a time for martyrs now. And if I'm to
be one, it will be in the cause of brotherhood.'*

Freed from the inflexible Nation of
Islam, Malcolm X used his trip abroad
to learn about true Islam. He was
surprised to find that he knew none
of the correct Islamic rituals, not even
how to pray. The whole experience
was an inspiration to him since his

disillusion with Elijah Muhammad's Islam. He marvelled at the sense of brotherhood at Mecca's Great Mosque, where people of all colours – even the blond-haired, blue-eyed 'White devils' – were united under Allah. He realized he may have been unfair to think of White people as inherently evil, and told the world's press on his return that he was prepared to judge them on their deeds. He said, 'I can get along with White people who can get along with me.' He celebrated his enlightenment by taking an Islamic name: El-Hajj Malik El-Shabazz.

He was invited to many countries which had just been released from the yoke of European imperialism, where he met some of his idols, such as President Nkrumah of Ghana, and the founder of modern Kenya, Jomo Kenyatta. Seeing the need to promote Black consciousness throughout the world, he founded the Organization of Afro-American Unity on his return. In his absence, America had erupted into the violence of the 'long, hot summer' of 1964. With revised opinions, Malcolm X joined forces with the more moderate Black leaders who had once not been prepared even to speak to him. His new organization needed money, and he travelled the world again on a fund-raising expedition. His popularity worldwide led to so many invitations to speak that he extended his stay.

But the net was closing in. French intelligence uncovered a plot to kill him, and officials refused him entry to the country for fear of being hosts to an international disaster. He flew home from a series of lectures in London to find that his house in New York had been fire-bombed. A number of his closest associates had already been attacked and had begun to carry shotguns. He felt that the FBI had as much to do with the trouble and death threats as Muhammad and his supporters. He had always maintained that, like his father and grandfather before him, he would die by violence, and sensed that he would never read his autobiography in finished form.

Yet, as the world knew, Malcolm X was not the sort of person to give up. In fact, he sped up his campaign against oppression, working without sleep for days. On Sunday, 21 February 1965, at Harlem's Audobon Ballroom, Malcolm X was due to make his weekly speech. Ironically, he had ordered his guards not to search the audience, saying, 'If I can't be safe among my own kind, where can I be?' At 2 p.m. the crowd assembled, and Malcolm warmly greeted them. A scuffle in the audience diverted his attention for a second: 'Let's cool it, brothers . . .' He probably did not see the three men in the front row who stood and took aim, pumping volleys of lead into his defenceless body like a firing-squad. As the first sixteen shotgun pellets found their target, Malcolm's hands flew into the air, his middle finger blown clean away. Like a huge marble statue, he stiffly toppled backwards, his head crashing heavily on the stage floor.

In the panic of screaming and gunshots, Malcolm's assistants ran to his aid, while his assailants fled the hall. Before anyone could help, he was dead, aged only thirty-nine.

One murderer, Talmadge Hayer, was captured outside the Ballroom, and, in the following days, his two accomplices were also caught. They were never linked to the Nation of Islam, nor any other group, and the identity of those who arranged Malcolm's assassination remains a mystery.

Fortunately, Malcolm's message continued to reach the world with the help of his remarkable autobiography. He had started to dictate his life story to Alex Haley years before his murder. Shortly after his funeral, the book was ready for publication. Malcolm X has endured as the world's most famous Black leader. It is to his credit that his murderers' bullets only made him a legend. His ceaseless, dedicated and uncompromising battle for racial justice has inspired millions across the world to continue the fight in his absence.

FURTHER MINI SERIES
INCLUDE

THEY DIED TOO YOUNG

Elvis
James Dean
Buddy Holly
Jimi Hendrix
Sid Vicious
Marc Bolan
Ayrton Senna
Marilyn Monroe
Jim Morrison

THEY DIED TOO YOUNG

Malcolm X
Kurt Cobain
River Phoenix
John Lennon
Glenn Miller
Isadora Duncan
Rudolph Valentino
Freddie Mercury
Bob Marley

FURTHER MINI SERIES
INCLUDE

HEROES OF THE WILD WEST

General Custer
Butch Cassidy and the Sundance Kid
Billy the Kid
Annie Oakley
Buffalo Bill
Geronimo
Wyatt Earp
Doc Holliday
Sitting Bull
Jesse James